W9-AGI-486

VERY IMPORTANT PEOPLE

MAHALIA JACKSON

Freedom's Voice

DENISE LEWIS PATRICK

INTERIOR ILLUSTRATIONS BY
JEN BRICKING

HARPER
An Imprint of HarperCollinsPublishers

www.harpercollinschildrens.com

Library of Congress Control Number: 2020952879

ISBN 978-0-06-288968-3 (pbk) — ISBN 978-0-06-297809-7

Illustrations by Jen Bricking

Typography by Torborg Davern

21 22 23 24 25   PC/LSCC   10 9 8 7 6 5 4 3 2 1

❖

First Edition

For Gail

Contents

Prologue

No one believed that such a crowd would show up that hot August day in 1963. The famous gospel singer Mahalia Jackson had come to Washington, DC, because her good friend Reverend Martin Luther King Jr. asked her to.

She had come because this day was special. From the moment she'd met the young reverend years ago, she'd believed in his message—that African Americans should speak out, sit in, and march to protest prejudice and unfair treatment. Now people from all over the United States and the world had gathered for the March on Washington for Jobs and Freedom.

They believed that all Americans deserved good jobs, good schools, and equal rights.

She had come to help bring people together. As Reverend King sat nearby, she stood and grabbed the sides of the microphone stand.

She had come to sing.

"I've been 'buked, and I've been scorned . . ." She began to sing slowly. Her voice rose powerfully, fell to a soft tone, and then rose again. The crowd recognized the words. They came from an old song once sung by enslaved people, and they meant, "I've been treated badly, and I've been ignored."

When Mahalia Jackson sat back down, Martin Luther King Jr. smiled at her. A few minutes later he was at the podium. Everyone, including Mahalia, listened with excitement as he began.

"Tell them about the dream, Martin!" she shouted. Then her friend gave the most unforgettable speech of his career.

"I have a dream!" he preached. Mahalia clapped and cheered.

She remembered being a poor little girl growing up in New Orleans. She'd dreamed of a better life for herself. She'd dreamed that her incredible voice was a gift she could use to make life better for other African Americans. At that moment, she knew that she had come to the March on Washington because Martin's dream was her dream, too.

CHAPTER 1

Growing Up by the Riverside

New Orleans, Louisiana, was a big, busy city in 1912. Boats and barges of all sizes ran up and down the Mississippi River, carrying everything from bananas

to coal. Workers on the docks sang and sweated as they loaded and unloaded cargo. Musicians and singers in the city's famous French Quarter entertained visitors from all over the world. In one neighborhood along the river, near the levee that held the waters of the mighty Mississippi back, the Clark family welcomed a new member. A baby girl was born to Charity Clark and Johnny Jackson on October 26. She was named after one of her mother's sisters, Mahalia.

Baby Mahalia wasn't healthy at first. Haley, as her family called her, was born with eye problems. Her legs were not straight. Doctors told her mother that she might need surgery to correct them. Mahalia's parents didn't have the money for that.

Many African American women like Charity Clark and her sisters worked as maids or cooks for wealthier white families. Johnny and Charity weren't married. He lived with his parents. During the day he worked one job as a stevedore, loading and unloading ships on the docks. He also worked part-time as a barber and a preacher.

When Haley's mother had to go back to work, the Clark family stepped in to help take care of Haley. Her aunts rubbed and massaged the baby's legs and fed her healthy food. As she grew, Mahalia recovered. She and her older brother, Peter, had aunts, uncles, and cousins all around. Soon, the bright, curious little girl was a lively part of her family and her community.

Like Haley's family, their neighbors were all poor working people. Everyone knew each other. Many families grew their own vegetables in small gardens. The children played together. But their big excitement wasn't school or the playground. For them, the riverfront was the place to be.

Sometimes they watched the trains traveling upriver to and from the nearby coal yard. When they waved to get the engineers' attention, the trains would often stop to give them a ride on the engine or caboose. Those rides came with sweet treats, like sugarcane. After a quick trip, it was back home again!

At other times, Mahalia gathered with the neighborhood children by the levee. They collected driftwood from the riverbanks to make campfires.

One boy played a ukulele, while everyone sang as they snacked on pecans and baked sweet potatoes.

Even as a small girl, Mahalia loved singing and tried to repeat from memory any song that she heard. She sang in the children's choir at church, too. The congregation at Plymouth Rock Baptist Church knew that Mahalia Jackson had a great big voice. Haley felt good inside when they clapped and swayed and sang along with her.

However, when Mahalia was only five years old, her mother, Charity, suddenly died. What would happen to Mahalia and Peter? Where would they go?

The Clarks made an important decision. While they agreed to let Haley visit her father and his family, they determined that she and her brother would live with one of their aunts. The children only had to move a few blocks away. Mahalia and Emmanuel Paul took them in. Haley shared her aunt's name, but everyone called the grown-up Mahalia "Duke."

Mahalia's life changed without her mother. She missed Charity's love and encouragement. Aunt Duke had different ideas about

children. Mahalia soon discovered that her days of carefree playing were over.

Aunt Duke taught her to dust the furniture, scrub the floors, and iron clothes. She had to make sure there was enough wood and coal in the house for cooking and heating. Since music was already an important part of Mahalia's life, she hummed while she did the chores. When she was old enough to attend school, she got in trouble with her teachers because she hummed songs in the classroom, too.

By the time she was about seven, young Mahalia went to work alongside a relative, like many poor children in the 1920s.

For a few years, the little girl with the big voice went every morning with one of her teenage aunts to work for a white family. Before they went to their own school, they washed dishes and helped the children in the house get ready for school. Mahalia and her aunt Bessie went back to the job after their school day ended. Although Haley liked earning two dollars a week and getting "hand-me-down dresses," life wasn't easy for her or her family.

"Things were pretty lean," she said years later. "I had this feeling that I could live better." Racial discrimination kept many Black people in New Orleans from living better lives. Laws separated Black people from white people in restaurants, hotels, and on streetcars. According to these Jim Crow laws, children went to all-Black or all-white schools, no matter which was closer.

Mahalia thought of becoming a nurse when she grew up. But no one in her family had much education or a professional career. As she tried to figure out the challenges of school and work and becoming a teenager, she discovered her cousin Fred's record collection.

Fred was Aunt Duke's son. He was already a young man who worked on the docks near the river. One day when he was out, Mahalia sneaked into his room and cranked up his Victrola record player. That day, a whole new world of music opened up to her. She heard the blues and jazz for the first time. This music was very different from church music.

Pretty soon, Mahalia realized that her new music world would cause big trouble for her in Aunt Duke's world. Fred's music was called "the blues."

Music in New Orleans: Feeling the Blues

The early blues style of music grew from African American story-songs, called *ballads*, and the work chants of enslaved African Americans in the fields of the South. This new music was not like that sung by most church choirs or played on church organs. At church, often there was only a guitar player and a vocalist, singing words about the hardships of life.

As the blues became more popular, those performers appeared at dances and in night-clubs. When the recording industry grew, the blues spread across the country and the world. Many performers became famous, like piano player and composer W. C. Handy, guitarist Robert Johnson, and Mahalia's favorite—singer Bessie Smith. Mahalia said Bessie Smith's voice had more "soul" than any of the other female blues singers at the time.

CHAPTER 2

Aunt Duke's World

In Aunt Duke's world, rules were important. One of her rules was that her niece only sing and listen to church music. That's why Mahalia waited until her aunt was out to listen to Fred's records.

Aunt Duke called it "the devil's music." But Mahalia was curious. She realized that hearing the blues and dancing to jazz made some people feel good, just like the hymns she sang in church made her feel.

What made people react that way? Mahalia wondered. Was it the way the musicians played? Was it the words of the songs, or how the singers sang them? Or was it all those things? Without knowing it, she was studying music.

When she went to Mount Moriah Baptist Church with Aunt Duke, Mahalia sang the slow, serious hymns that the people liked. But near their house was a different church. Mahalia often heard their services, too. The way that their choir sang hymns was not the same. Their singing had a lively, powerful beat. It was loud. In addition to piano music, there were drums and tambourines. The people were so moved by the music that they even danced during the service!

Mahalia's voice continued to gain strength and power. As she grew up, she began to try singing hymns in a new way. She wanted to blend the beat and rhythm of blues with the words of old church hymns. She wanted to create something new. Mount Moriah didn't really like it, and Aunt Duke didn't, either.

Aunt Duke's rules kept Mahalia busy even when she wasn't working or going to school. By the time she reached eighth grade, Mahalia had learned to iron a man's shirt in only three minutes.

She could do laundry as well as a grown woman could. She knew that she could earn good money to help the family if she worked full-time. So, although she'd once dreamed of getting a real education, Mahalia quit school. She worked hard, ten hours a day.

But teenage Mahalia soon found out that having a job and her own money didn't free her from Aunt Duke's rules. Mahalia said years later that she understood that her aunt only wanted to keep her out of trouble. However, Mahalia was just as interested in life and music as she'd always been. She was ready to explore the excitement of New Orleans.

One of the first times Mahalia and her aunt had a falling-out was during Mardi Gras. Every year, the entire city of New Orleans celebrated the carnival called Mardi Gras. This was a time of music and parades in the streets. Aunt Duke had given Mahalia a curfew—a special time to be back home. Mahalia got home late one night, and Aunt Duke was angry. She wouldn't open the door, so Mahalia had to spend the night with another relative.

Another time, Mahalia and a cousin went to a party. The crowd got rowdy, and a young man attacked Mahalia's cousin, Celie. Their friends tried to remind Mahalia about her curfew, but she thought it was more important to protect her cousin. She got into a fight with the man. Aunt Duke was so furious that she told Mahalia not to return. Mahalia decided then that she would never go back.

At barely fifteen years old, Mahalia was on her own. With help from another aunt, she found a tiny house in the neighborhood. She used money she'd earned at her job to rent the place for six dollars a month. Things were tough. Mahalia thought of trying to make a living from singing, but she wasn't sure she could be successful.

She knew that chances for a better life in New Orleans were slim. She was African American and poor. Even if she had a good education, the Jim Crow laws all over the South would limit her future. Mahalia decided to leave New Orleans. She used money she'd saved to buy a train ticket.

Some of her Clark uncles and aunts had already gone up north to Chicago, where they earned higher wages and told the New Orleans family about how much better things were for Black people. When her aunt Hannah came to visit New Orleans for Thanksgiving in 1927, Mahalia was ready. She packed up her few belongings, her hopes, and her dreams. And when Aunt Hannah boarded the train back to Chicago, Mahalia was with her.

The Great Migration

While there were many African Americans who stood up against Jim Crow laws, and some white people who tried to help them, these laws made life dangerous and difficult. States passed special laws to prevent African Americans from voting. Black people were beaten, threatened, or unfairly arrested. In some towns and communities, the homes, churches, or businesses of African Americans were burned down. Many families were forced to make the hard choice to leave their lives in the South behind for good.

Up to one million African Americans left in the years between 1915 and 1970. This "Great Migration" spread the African American population across much of the country. During the years between 1910 and 1920, African American communities in

northern cities such as Chicago, Detroit, and Pittsburgh grew more than twice as large. In these cities and others, Black workers could often find jobs where they earned more money than they could in the South. They could vote, and live more freely in public.

The move wasn't trouble-free for everyone who made it. Even in northern and western cities, some African Americans faced unfair treatment and discrimination. Still, the Great Migration was important in shaping the way many of our vibrant cities and communities look today.

CHAPTER 3

A New Home

The train ride to Chicago took almost a full day. Mahalia wasn't ready for the cold northern winter at all—she didn't even have a coat. But the weather wasn't the only thing that was surprising about her new home.

At the station, Aunt Hannah got into a taxi with a white driver. Mahalia was shocked, because in New Orleans, almost everything had been segregated and separated. The taxi took them to her aunt's apartment building on the South Side.

The building seemed huge to Mahalia, compared to Aunt Duke's and the tiny house she'd just left. The apartment also felt big, even though Aunt

Hannah and Aunt Alice, her daughter Little Alice, other cousins, and a few boarders shared the space. Mahalia got a sleeping spot on a sofa and set out to find a job.

Chicago's South Side was then home to one of the largest African American communities in the United States. Unlike in some other cities, African Americans actually owned businesses. There were Black policemen and firefighters.

Calling Chicago Home

Chicago's South Side neighborhood has been home to many now-famous African Americans. Among them are former First Lady Michelle Obama, award-winning music composer and producer Quincy Jones, and musician Chance the Rapper. Film and TV writer Shonda Rhimes grew up in another Chicago neighborhood. Some well-known people who chose to make Chicago their home include artist and painter Kerry James Marshall, Oprah Winfrey, and former president Barack Obama. In fact, he met Michelle Obama while working in Chicago—that's why he stayed!

Mahalia was impressed by the way Black people in Chicago seemed to be moving forward. Here, she didn't have to go into the back doors of buildings or use separate water fountains from white people. She could sit wherever she wanted on the buses or the elevated trains. She quickly found a new church home at Greater Salem Baptist Church and became a lead singer with their choir.

At Greater Salem, Mahalia found a few friends who felt like family. They sang what Mahalia had grown to like, a combination of old hymns and blues rhythms called *gospel*. Mahalia and her new friends decided to form a singing group and called themselves the Johnson Gospel Singers. Once the word spread about how good the Johnson Gospel Singers

were, they got invited to sing at small churches all over the South Side. They made a little money at each performance. It wasn't much, because right around the time the group got together, the whole country was having money problems. It was called the Great Depression.

Banks closed suddenly. Big companies and factories laid off workers. Thousands of folks lost their jobs, so small neighborhood businesses began to close too. The South Side was hit hard—and like many other Americans, the African Americans who had built good lives in Chicago lost everything.

Somehow, in the middle of all these troubles, Mahalia and the Johnsons kept going. Black churches in nearby states began to ask for them. On weekends they traveled by car to Indiana and Ohio, and they even sang at the National Baptist Convention in Saint Louis, Missouri. One person who heard Mahalia in an early performance was a young African American gospel composer, Thomas A. Dorsey. They became friends. Dorsey was having a hard time getting listeners to connect with a different music style, as Mahalia had back home.

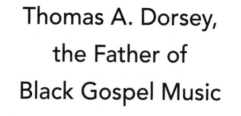

Thomas A. Dorsey, the Father of Black Gospel Music

Thomas Andrew Dorsey was born in Villa Roca, Georgia, in 1899. He was the son of a Baptist preacher and a church organist. He followed the Great Migration to Chicago as a young man, and played piano for blues singers and in jazz clubs. He is known as the creator of church music called gospel. At first, some churches didn't understand the way Dorsey's gospel music combined the beat of blues with words about hope and what he called "good news." It was so difficult for him to get choirs to perform gospel that for a time he went back to the blues.

In 1932, as Dorsey was on an out-of-town trip, he got horrible news: his wife, Nettie, and

their baby had both died. Filled with pain and sorrow, he sat down at his piano and thought of the words "Precious Lord, take my hand . . . lead me on, help me stand." Several years later, he began working with Mahalia Jackson. She sang "Take My Hand, Precious Lord" in her way, and audiences loved it. Encouraged, Dorsey went on to write more successful gospel songs—over four hundred in his lifetime.

At twenty years old, Mahalia's voice was getting attention well outside the Chicago area. She wasn't yet sure if singing gospel music could be a career, because some pastors still didn't think gospel sounded enough like church music. But at least she had a few dollars to give to her aunts to help with food and rent at the apartment.

The Johnson Singers' success didn't last long—and Mahalia soon found herself performing solo. She found other backup singers and musicians, and she decided to go on the road full-time. They traveled to

small churches as far as California and New York. Around Chicago, African Americans who'd left the South loved Mahalia Jackson, because to them, she sounded like home.

When a church invited her, she would often take a train and stay overnight with the pastor and his family. She ate meals with them. Audiences paid less than a dollar per ticket, and Mahalia shared part of her earnings with the churches. Sometimes she earned more than fifty dollars in one week. That was more than she'd get ironing shirts or working in a factory.

Mahalia had always thought of her voice as a gift given to her by God. Now she began to feel that it was her mission to share her gift with others. Gospel singing was becoming the most important thing in Mahalia's life. Her busy schedule didn't leave much time for her family or friends. During the late 1930s someone came along to change that.

On one of Mahalia's return trips to Chicago and to Greater Salem Baptist Church, she met a tall, intelligent man. His name was Isaac Hockenhull. He worked as a mail carrier for the post office. Mahalia liked that he was interested in music and that he was smart. He'd graduated from Tuskegee Institute, one of the few colleges for African Americans at the time.

But Mahalia was uneasy. She wasn't sure why such an educated man would like someone like her. Plus, she was only twenty-four, and he was ten years older. She agreed to be his friend. He took her out to dinner and bought her flowers. He even visited the South Side apartment to meet Aunt Hannah and Aunt Alice. They liked him.

Mahalia realized that she loved Ike, as she called

him. So, when he asked her to be his wife after they'd known each other about a year, she said yes. They were married in 1936.

In one way, it was a happy time for Mahalia. She liked being a wife, and when she was at home she loved cooking the delicious New Orleans food that she remembered. However, as the Depression dragged on, she didn't have so many singing jobs. She needed to make extra money, just like millions of others who worried they might not have enough to get by.

CHAPTER 4

Spreading Gospel Music

Not long after she got married, Mahalia was working at a local hotel as a maid when she got a call from a music producer in Chicago who'd heard her sing at the National Baptist Convention.

His company, Decca, was known for blues and jazz, but they wanted to hire Mahalia to make a gospel record. It had been almost ten years since young Haley Jackson had left New Orleans for Chicago. Now the girl who'd listened to her cousin Fred's records in secret would be able to make her own!

Mahalia went to Decca's studio in 1937 to record two songs. She had high hopes for their success, especially because gospel music was becoming more and more popular. But even though Decca was the third largest record company in the country,

Mahalia's records didn't sell very well. Mahalia was disappointed. Yet it seemed that each time her gospel career felt like it was failing, something happened to move her just a little higher.

Her old friend Thomas Dorsey was still touring with his music, putting together singers and choirs. The gospel music field was growing, and crowds were hungry for it.

Gospel Greats
and Gospel Roots

Mahalia Jackson and Thomas Dorsey weren't the only musicians who took up the new music known as gospel. In the 1940s, as gospel music spread across the country, other singers like Sister Rosetta Tharpe and

Clara Ward (along with her group, the Clara Ward Singers) became well known. By the 1950s and '60s, singers and musicians who started in gospel, such as Ray Charles, Sam Cooke, and Aretha Franklin, crossed over to popular rhythm and blues. Today, many original gospel favorites are still sung, along with church music in contemporary, rock, hip-hop, and even rap styles.

Dorsey had always liked the strength and power of Mahalia's voice, and he was looking for a singer. He wrote a song just for Mahalia called "Peace in the Valley," which later became one of her hits. Mahalia took the job Dorsey offered, leaving Ike unhappy at home.

Soon after, Ike lost his job, and Mahalia wasn't earning enough money singing. They struggled financially. The couple divorced in 1941.

Mahalia had to find a way to reach a larger audience with gospel. And again, something surprising happened! She was invited to give a gospel concert in New York City at a place called the Golden Gate Ballroom. The organizers offered to pay her

one thousand dollars! Mahalia had never earned or even heard of making that type of money for one appearance. Could a gospel singer draw a large enough crowd?

The answer, Mahalia found out, was *yes*. In the audience that evening was a woman who owned a small record company in New York called Apollo. She liked Mahalia's unique way of singing gospel so much that she asked her to come to a meeting the next day to discuss a record contract.

Mahalia's first song with Apollo, "I'm Gonna Tell God All About It One of These Days," came out a month later. Back in Chicago, a local radio DJ loved the song. He played it over and over on his jazz program. But not many people were as excited as he was by the record.

None of the other songs she recorded for Apollo sold well either. By the spring of 1947 Mahalia's contract was in danger of being canceled.

But Apollo's music director remembered something. While Mahalia had been practicing in the studio, she'd sung another song, "Move On Up a Little Higher." He called her.

She was on the road, but she told him she'd get back to New York to record the song again. On the new recording Mahalia performed the way she did onstage. She changed up the words. She added her blues style to the melody. The musicians kept right up with her changes. The director was satisfied.

"Move On Up" was released in December of 1947. In the Chicago area alone, the record sold fifty thousand copies in the first few weeks. New Orleans blues clubs played the gospel song by their hometown girl on their jukeboxes. Apollo had so many orders for records that they couldn't make them fast enough.

"Move On Up" was the first gospel hit record.

Mahalia was no longer a simple gospel singer. She was about to become an entertainer in show business.

Very soon, Mahalia would get a chance to discover the world—and how her music would help the Black community find its voice.

CHAPTER 5

Mahalia's Mission

In 1950, Mahalia was asked to participate in the first ever all-gospel program at New York's Carnegie Hall. The famous concert hall was known to be the home of opera singers and orchestras. That night, it was sold out. Mahalia was nervous about singing on a stage where such great artists had performed. She couldn't believe, she said, that "thousands of men and women . . . had come to hear me."

Once she began to sing, Mahalia forgot about her nerves. She gave a performance that brought the crowd to its feet, just like in church. The audience and the music critics loved her. That night, a writer from the *New York Times* called her "The Queen of Gospel Singers."

The New York Times.

"All the News That's Fit to Print"

THE WEATHER

VOL. XCIX..no 33,680   NEW YORK, OCTOBER 1950   5 CENTS

THE QUEEN OF GOSPEL SINGERS AT CARNEGIE HALL

Queen of Gospel Singers, Mahalia Jackson performs at Carnegie Hall, Oct. 1, 1950

The Carnegie Hall audience was mostly African American, but Mahalia's fame had spread outside the Black community, and even outside of America. She got word that a French music organization had given her an award. Mahalia and her team began making plans for her first European tour.

Mahalia wasn't sure how people in other countries would react to gospel if they couldn't understand the words. Since Mahalia was afraid to fly, she and her piano player Mildred Falls sailed to England.

She received greetings from England's Queen Elizabeth II and its prime minister, Winston Churchill. But the English audience just sat politely. Mahalia was used to audiences clapping and swaying, feeling the music and words with their bodies.

She was amazed that in France and Denmark, audiences cried as she sang, though they may not have understood any of the words. They *felt* them.

Then, at one of the last French concerts, Mahalia fainted backstage. It turned out that she needed surgery. Her remaining concerts were canceled, and she flew back to Chicago. Friends, fans, and her family were worried. After many months she was ready to sing again. As she recovered, she had lots of time to think.

One of the things she thought about was how warmly she'd been treated by white people in Europe. At one hotel, she had been greeted with a room full of flowers. People were kind to her and to Mildred, even though they were Black. Mahalia thought long and hard about why they weren't treated as nicely in some towns of their own country.

Just as she had helped change people's minds about gospel music, Mahalia thought the soulful music might change white Americans' hearts.

In 1953, Mahalia got her own local radio show. At the time, not many African Americans appeared on television, and there weren't many African Americans who hosted radio shows. Here was her chance to bring gospel to a wider audience. *The Mahalia Jackson Show* was first broadcast September 26, 1954, and she made several appearances on Ed Sullivan's Sunday evening variety program. She was also a guest more than once on singer Nat King Cole's program. Cole was the first African American to have a national television show.

As busy as she was, Mahalia always made time

to sing at the National Baptist Convention, where she'd first gotten noticed so long ago. She attended the convention in Denver in 1956. There, she met two young preachers. One was named Ralph Abernathy, and the other was named Martin Luther King Jr.

Mahalia listened to King's message of protesting unfairness without using violence. She saw that he had a mission in his life very much like her own, to change people's hearts. Over the next several years Mahalia and Martin became close friends.

Brown v. Board of Education: The Beginning of the Civil Rights Movement

By the 1940s and 1950s, Jim Crow laws had affected education all over the South. Some people believed that schools for Black students were separate but equal to schools that white children attended, but that was not always true. In many towns and cities (and not only southern ones), African American students attended all-Black schools even if a white school was closer. Many Black schools had only old, outdated books and badly kept buildings. Parents felt their children weren't getting an equal chance to learn.

Over several years, Black parents filed lawsuits against the US government to try to solve this problem. Finally, the case, called *Brown v. Board of Education of Topeka*, made its way to the highest court in America, the US Supreme Court. In 1954, the Supreme Court ruled that the "separate but equal" laws were not fair. The court decided that schools and universities had to be open to all students. Many white people opposed the change. They threw things at Black students, called them ugly names, and even spit at them. Some Black students in Little Rock, Arkansas, needed police protection just to attend high school. But the ruling encouraged African Americans to openly challenge other unjust laws. In many ways, it opened the door to the civil rights movement.

A few weeks after the Baptist Convention, Ralph Abernathy invited Mahalia to come down to Montgomery, Alabama, to sing at a rally. In December of 1955, a Montgomery woman named Rosa Parks had refused to give her seat to a white passenger on a city bus. That was the law in Montgomery. Parks was arrested. Her action had started a boycott in the city.

Abernathy, King, and other civil rights leaders persuaded African American citizens to stop riding the buses in protest. Their efforts had been successful for months, and the rally was a way to convince people to continue the boycott.

Mahalia instantly said yes and headed south. She had faced discrimination many times over the years as she and Mildred had driven to and from concerts. They had been refused service at restaurants when they were hungry. Often, they had to drive for hours late at night because some hotels wouldn't allow African Americans to stay.

Mahalia knew how important the Montgomery bus boycott could be.

In Montgomery she stayed overnight with Reverend Abernathy and his family, just as she had in her early singing days. They welcomed her and shared meals.

Mahalia performed and then returned to Chicago. Two nights after she arrived home she received a disturbing telephone call. Ralph Abernathy's home had been bombed by people who wanted to stop the boycott.

No one was hurt, but Mahalia was very upset by the news. Perhaps, in a way, it prepared her for what came next in her own life.

Mahalia began looking for a house in Chicago. In the apartment building where she lived, some tenants were not happy hearing her practice music quite so much. It didn't matter that Mahalia also

owned the building. She needed a house, not an apartment. She began looking. Her search took her out of the South Side. She found a house that she liked in a different part of the city. It was large, and brick, set apart from the others.

Mahalia found out there was a problem. She was an African American woman who wanted to buy a house in a white neighborhood of Chicago. It didn't matter that she was a famous gospel singer, or that she had the money. No white person would sell to her. Mahalia was outraged. She was determined to get what she wanted.

She finally found a white doctor who would sell his house to her. The neighbors held meetings about it and sent threatening notes. Mahalia never changed her plans to move in. But before she could, someone fired shots into the front windows one night. Mahalia called the mayor of Chicago, whom she knew. He sent a police car to sit outside. A police car came every

night for weeks, even after she moved in.

Mahalia's experience and what happened to the Abernathy family helped her begin to think differently about her gospel mission. This was just the kind of unfairness King was trying to fight. She was ready to do even more to help. Often, Martin would call her late at night when he was troubled. They had long talks, and he'd sometimes ask her to sing gospel songs to him over the telephone. Even if they were both on the road, Mahalia always did. It seemed that in her voice, and gospel music itself, King found a special strength. That was the power Mahalia planned to spread to gospel listeners everywhere.

CHAPTER 6

The Voice of a Nation

By 1959 Mahalia was well known to Black and white audiences across the United States and all over the world. Although she had helped one or two African Americans in Chicago get elected to public office, she'd never been very involved with politics. That changed when she was invited to sing at the White House for President Dwight Eisenhower and First Lady Mamie Eisenhower. Mahalia was honored.

There was a presidential election the following year, 1960. President Eisenhower was not running again, but a young man from Massachusetts was. His name was John F. Kennedy, and he won.

A big party was planned the night before his

inauguration, or swearing-in ceremony. Once again, Mahalia was asked to sing for a president. This time the special request was a song Mahalia had never sung before. It was "The Star-Spangled Banner," America's national anthem.

After the performance, there was a formal dinner. Mahalia was sitting at her table when she looked up to see John F. Kennedy coming toward her. He thanked her and shook her hand.

In that moment, she decided that she liked the new president. If he was willing to shake the hand of a Black woman, she thought he just might be the leader the country needed to survive its troubled times.

"It Ought to Be Possible . . ."

Before and after his 1960 election, John F. Kennedy spoke out against separating Black and white students in schools and universities. He encouraged businesses to treat African Americans fairly. Kennedy's actions gave African Americans hope. But many cities and states were slow to change.

In 1962, James Meredith tried to attend the University of Mississippi. White students rioted to keep him out. Many people were injured and two people died. The president had to send National Guard troops to protect Meredith. The next year in Birmingham, Alabama, officials used police dogs and firehoses to stop Black student protests. Many of those students were children. The violence was shown on TV around the world. President Kennedy sent thousands of

troops to help settle things peacefully.

After the governor of Alabama also refused to allow two Black students to enroll at the University of Alabama, Kennedy decided it was time to address the nation. He spoke on June 11, 1963.

"It ought to be possible," he said, "for American students of any color to attend any public institution they select . . . It ought to be possible for American citizens of any

color to register and to vote . . . without inter-
ference or fear . . ."

He called on communities across the
country to "see right." He urged Congress
to pass a new law to end racial discrimination and protect the equal rights of African
Americans. However, Kennedy did not live to
see change happen. He was assassinated
on November 22, 1963. Lyndon B. Johnson

became the next president, and he worked with Congress to push the new law through. The Civil Rights Act was passed on July 2, 1964.

In 1962, the National Academy of Recording Arts and Sciences, the organization that gave out the special music awards called the Grammys, decided to give their first ever award for gospel singing. They chose to award it to Mahalia Jackson. Despite the growing number of new, young gospel singers and musicians, she won the Grammy again in 1963.

As busy as she was with touring all around the world, Mahalia never forgot about the civil rights struggle. The country was facing deepening racial troubles. Encouraged by the Brown court decision to desegregate schools and colleges, African Americans were making their voices heard on other types of discrimination.

They called on President Kennedy and Congress to pass new laws to help protect their voting rights. They had "sit-ins" at restaurants and lunch counters that refused Black customers. Martin Luther King and others organized marches for fair housing. Yet, in many southern cities and towns, nonviolent protesters were met with guns, water hoses, and police dogs.

In August of 1963, King and other leaders had organized a big protest march. They hoped that

lawmakers—and the president—might pay attention if a large enough group came out to support equal rights and justice for all Americans. He asked his friend to sing again.

The plan was for people to gather at the Washington Monument and walk up to the Lincoln Memorial at the other end of the Washington Mall. There, in front of the giant statue of Abraham Lincoln, many people would demand equality for Black Americans.

The March on Washington for Jobs and Freedom

By 1963 African Americans had been fighting for over fifty years for equal rights as citizens. They wanted voting rights, fair pay in jobs, and good schools for their children. There had been nonviolent protest marches, like those led by Martin Luther King Jr. and others. Students, both Black and white, sat down at lunch counters and restaurants that refused

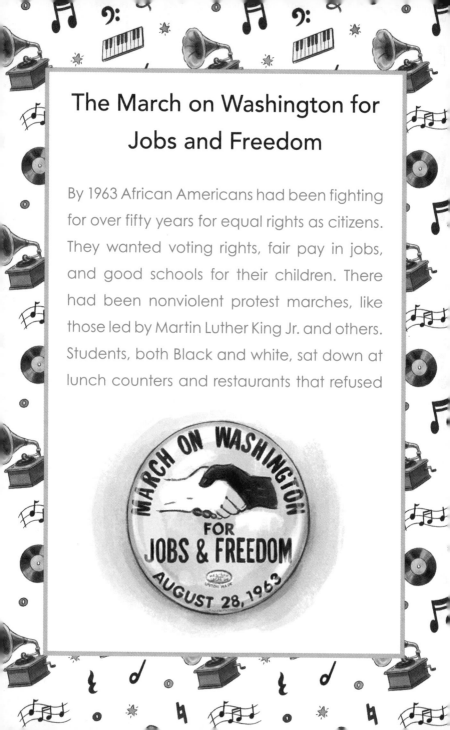

to serve Black people. A group of civil rights leaders came up with the idea of a gathering in Washington, DC, to encourage more people to support justice and equality.

They began arriving in the morning, though the program didn't officially begin until afternoon. When it did, people were shoulder to shoulder along the length of the Mall. To the surprise of many, an estimated 250,000 people showed up.

There were preachers and rabbis, teachers and garbage collectors. There were college students and children and grandparents. There were people from Canada and Europe. And along with so many ordinary people, many famous Hollywood stars, musicians, and entertainers joined the march.

Mahalia Jackson performed near the end of the day, just before Martin Luther King Jr.

Mahalia had come because this day was special. She had come to bring people together. From the moment she'd met the young reverend years ago, she'd believed in his message—that Black Americans deserved good jobs, good schools, and equal rights.

Now people from all over the United States and the world had gathered to show that they believed the message, too.

As Reverend King sat nearby, she stood and grabbed the sides of the microphone stand.

"I've been 'buked, and I've been scorned . . ." She began to sing slowly. Her voice rose powerfully, fell to a soft tone, and then rose again. The crowd recognized the words. They came from an old song once sung by enslaved people, and they meant, "I've been treated badly, and I've been ignored."

The people began to cheer and whistle as she finished. Their clapping was like thunder. They didn't want Mahalia to leave the stage. They wanted an *encore*—one more song. She sang "How I Got Over."

That day, Mahalia Jackson truly seemed to be the voice of the nation.

A few minutes later her old friend Martin was at the podium. Everyone, including the woman whose gospel music had thrilled audiences in Paris, France, and Germany, listened with excitement as he began.

"Tell them about the dream, Martin!" she shouted. Then her friend gave the most unforgettable speech of his career.

"I have a dream!" he preached. Mahalia clapped and cheered him as he spoke of his hope that Black and white children might one day live together as friends. She was filled with pride.

At that moment, she remembered being a poor little girl growing up in New Orleans. She'd dreamed of a better life for herself. She'd dreamed that her incredible voice was a gift she could use to make life better for other African Americans. She knew then that she had come to the March on Washington because Martin's dream was her dream, too.

CHAPTER 7

"Troubles of the World"

Only a few weeks after the march, four African American girls were killed when a church was bombed in Birmingham, Alabama. The violent act made news worldwide, but it did not stop the civil rights movement or the protests. Then, on November 22, 1963, President Kennedy was shot and killed during a motorcade in Dallas, Texas.

The world was shocked. Mahalia had high hopes that Kennedy could unite the country. She was on the road in California when she heard. She was shaken. CBS put together a special program to air live on national TV. Mahalia sang and cried as if she'd lost a friend.

The Dallas Morning News

VOL. 115—No. 54   DALLAS, TEXAS, SATURDAY, NOVEMBER 23, 1963   PRICE 5 CENTS

KENNEDY SLAIN ON DALLAS STREET
★ ★ ★ ★   ★ ★ ★ ★   ★ ★ ★ ★
JOHNSON BECOMES PRESIDENT

On an earlier trip to California Mahalia had met Sigmund Galloway, who played flute in an orchestra. He had family ties in Indiana, where she had performed many times over the years. He was interested in her career and attended many of her concerts. Sigmund began to spend more time with Mahalia after 1963, maybe helping to take her mind off the sadness she felt. Her agent and friends noticed.

Mahalia and Sigmund got married in 1964, though their relationship did not last long. Sigmund wanted his own music career, and had trouble accepting Mahalia's success. The marriage broke up.

It wasn't long before Mahalia had another awful blow. Martin Luther King Jr. was killed in Memphis, Tennessee, on April 4, 1968. He had gone to Memphis to support a strike by sanitation workers there. A man shot him while he was standing on the balcony outside his motel room. Many African American communities reacted to the death of this nonviolent leader with riots and violent clashes with police.

Of all the hardships Mahalia had experienced, this was one of the hardest. King had left behind his wife, Coretta Scott King, who was expecting a baby, and three children. Coretta was also a friend. She asked Mahalia to sing at the funeral.

Coretta Scott King:
Leading in Her Own Way

When Coretta Scott met Martin Luther King Jr., she was studying singing at the New England Conservatory of Music. After they married in 1953, Coretta's life as a pastor's wife and mother kept her busy. However, as the struggle for equal rights continued, she found her own way to help.

Coretta got the idea to use her musical skills to perform "Freedom Concerts" across the country. She sang, recited poetry, and spoke to audiences about the civil rights movement. She often traveled with her husband when he went to other countries like Ghana and India to meet with world leaders. She also marched alongside him in many nonviolent protests across the South.

Martin Luther King Jr. was shot and killed in Memphis, Tennessee, on April 4, 1968. He'd planned to march with workers the next day. As hard as it was, Coretta marched in his place. From then on, she continued to work for freedom. She helped start the Martin Luther King Jr. Center for Nonviolent Social Change in Atlanta, Georgia. And she played an important role in getting Congress to approve a holiday in Dr. King's honor. Martin Luther King Day was first observed as a national holiday in 1986.

Coretta Scott King spent the rest of her life working for peace, racial equality, and fair treatment for women and children around the world. She died in 2006.

Mahalia honored Martin Luther King Jr. with "Take My Hand," Thomas A. Dorsey's song of sorrow.

Shortly after the death of King, Mahalia set up a foundation in Chicago to give scholarships to college students. She also had dreams of raising money to build a place of worship that all people could attend. She continued to tour, including a trip through Asia in 1971. In Japan she sang for Emperor Hirohito, and in India she met Prime Minister Indira Gandhi.

In late 1971 officials in Washington, DC, asked her to visit US army bases in Germany. There had been trouble between Black and white soldiers. Once again, Mahalia saw the chance to bring people together through song. However, after she arrived, she began having trouble with her heart and was flown home urgently on a military plane.

Not long after returning, Mahalia Jackson died in a Chicago hospital on January 27, 1972. She was sixty years old.

EPILOGUE

Going Home

Greater Salem Baptist Church in Chicago held a viewing the day before Mahalia's memorial service. Over a full day, more than forty thousand friends and fans came to the church to show respect for the "Queen of Gospel."

Some six thousand people attended the memorial service at the McCormick Place Convention Center in Chicago. Coretta Scott King spoke, telling the crowd, "The causes of justice, freedom, and brotherhood have lost a real champion." Thomas A. Dorsey did a reading. US president Richard M. Nixon sent a message calling Mahalia an "ambassador of goodwill." And young Aretha Franklin, who began her career singing gospel in her father's church, sang "Take My Hand."

Mahalia's body was then taken to her first home, New Orleans, for a final service and burial.

She once said in an interview that when she was a girl, she "thought way in the beyond, in the future." Over her sixty years of life Mahalia Jackson worked, and sometimes fought, to make her own future.

She helped audiences learn to love and accept gospel music. She worked to help make a better future for African Americans. She believed in a future for her country. And all along, she stayed true to her mission: to use the gift of her incredible voice and heart to help others.

MAHALIA JACKSON
OCTOBER 26, 1912
JANUARY 27, 1972
"THE WORLD'S GREATEST GOSPEL SINGER"

Timeline: Mahalia Jackson

1911
Mahalia Jackson is born in New Orleans, Louisiana

1916?
Charity Clark, Mahalia's mother, dies

1927
Mahalia leaves for Chicago with Aunt Hannah

1937
Mahalia records two gospel songs with Decca and goes on the road with Thomas A. Dorsey

1941
The United States enters WWII; Mahalia and Isaac divorce

1946
Mahalia records her first four songs with Apollo Records in New York

1953
Mahalia leaves Apollo Records, signs with Columbia Records

1954
The Mahalia Jackson Show is first broadcast on radio in Chicago

1955
Rosa Parks refuses to give up her bus seat; the Montgomery, Alabama, bus boycott begins

1929
The Johnson Gospel
Singers form

1932
Thomas A. Dorsey
writes "Take My Hand"

1936
Mahalia and Isaac
Hockenhull marry

1947
Mahalia records
"Move On Up" with
Apollo

1950
Mahalia sings at
Carnegie Hall

1952
Mahalia's first
European tour to
England, France,
Holland, Belgium,
and Denmark;
Mahalia becomes ill

1956
Mahalia meets Martin
Luther King Jr. and Ralph
Abernathy at the National
Baptist Convention

1956
Mahalia sings at a
rally to support the
Montgomery bus
boycott

Timeline:
Mahalia Jackson

1959
President Dwight D. Eisenhower invites Mahalia to sing at the White House for the first time

1961
Mahalia's second European tour, including the Holy Land

1962
Mahalia receives the first Grammy for gospel music

1964
Mahalia and Sigmund Galloway marry

1965
President Lyndon B. Johnson invites Mahalia to the White House

1972
Mahalia dies on January 27, 1972

1963
Mahalia sings at the March on Washington for Jobs and Freedom

1963
Sixteenth Street Church is bombed in Birmingham, Alabama; four girls are killed

1963
President John F. Kennedy Jr. is shot and killed in Dallas, Texas

1968
Martin Luther King Jr. is shot and killed in Memphis, Tennessee

1971
Mahalia tours Asia and meets the emperor of Japan and prime minister of India

1971
Mahalia visits army bases in Germany; she falls ill

VIP Hall of Fame

Mahalia Jackson is one of many Black female singers and musicians who became activists and championed important antiracist causes. Here are a few more you should know about!

Marian Anderson was an award-winning vocalist who faced injustice and prejudice, along with many other Black artists, during the Jim Crow era. In 1939, after an organization would not give her permission to perform because she was

Black, Marian sang for a crowd of 75,000 at the Lincoln Memorial, with the support of President Franklin D. Roosevelt and First Lady Eleanor Roosevelt.

H.E.R. is the stage name of Gabriella Wilson, a Black and Filipina singer, songwriter, and activist. Her award-winning 2020 song "I Can't Breathe" demands an end to police brutality toward Black and brown people in the U.S. while calling out the privileged people who enable it.

Nina Simone was a classical pianist and celebrated jazz icon and a powerful member of the civil rights movement. Her song "To Be Young, Gifted, and Black" became an anthem during the late 1960s, and she often performed at rallies, including the Selma to Montgomery marches.

 **Sister Souljah** is a hip-hop artist, political commentator, and activist who held concerts and protests against racial discrimination and violence in the 1980s. She is also a writer, and her debut novel, *The Coldest Winter Ever*, was a bestseller.

Bibliography

Appiah, Kwame Anthony, and Henry Louis Gates, eds. *Africana: The Encyclopedia of the African and African American Experience.* New York: Basic Civitas Books, 1999.

Applebome, Peter. "Coretta Scott King, a Civil Rights Icon, Dies at 78." *New York Times*, February 1, 2006. https://www.nytimes.com/2006/02/01/obituaries/coretta-scott-king-a-civil-rights-icon-dies-at-78.html.

Blackpast. "African American History Timeline." Last accessed July 11, 2019. https://blackpast.org/timelines/african-american-history-timeline-1900-2000.

Ginger Group. "Clara Ward Singers." *American Roots Music*. PBS series. 2001. https://www.pbs.org/americanrootsmusic/pbs_arm_saa_clarawardsingers.html.

Grossman, Ron. "Mahalia Jackson, 'Queen of Gospel' to Chicago and the World." *Chicago Tribune*, September 13, 2018. https://www.chicagotribune.com/news/opinion/commentary/ct-perspec-flashback-mahalia-jackson-gospel-0916-20180912-story.html.

Haddad, Lulie, producer. "Episode 3: Guide My Feet." *This Far by Faith*. 2003. Coproduction of Blackside Inc. and The Faith Project, Inc. in association with the Independent Television Service. https://www.pbs.org/thisfarbyfaith/about/episode_3.html and https://vimeo.com/170417727.

Hughes, Langston, Milton Meltzer, and C. Eric Lincoln, eds. *A Pictoral History of Black Americans*. 5th ed. New York: Crown: 1983.

Jackson, Mahalia. *I Sing Because I'm Happy.* Interview with songs. Recorded, compiled, and annotated by Jules Schwerin. Smithsonian Folkways Recordings, 1995.

Jackson, Mahalia, with Evan McLeod Wylie. *Movin' On Up.* New York: Hawthorn Books, 1966.

John F. Kennedy Presidential Library and Museum. "Civil Rights Movement." JFK in History. Last accessed July 11, 2019. https://www.jfklibrary.org/learn/about-jfk/jfk-in-history/ civil-rights-movement.

Johnson, Jerah. "Jim Crow Laws of the 1890s and the Origins of New Orleans Jazz: Correction of an Error." *Popular Music* 19, no. 2 (2000): 243–51. www.jstor.org/stable/853671.

King Center. "About Mrs. King." Last accessed July 11, 2019. http://thekingcenter.org/about-mrs-king.

King, Martin Luther, Jr. "Address at the Freedom Rally in Cobo Hall." Transcript of speech c. June 23, 1963. The Martin Luther King, Jr. Research and Education Institute. Stanford University. https://kinginstitute.stanford.edu/king-papers/ documents/address-freedom-rally-cobo-hall.

Kramer, Barbara. *Mahalia Jackson: The Voice of Gospel and Civil Rights.* Berkeley Heights, NJ: Enslow Publishers, 2003.

Library of Congress. "Today in History - October 26: Mahalia Jackson." Last accessed July 11, 2019. http://www.loc.gov/ item/today-in-history/October-26/.

McKenzie, Margo. "Thomas Dorsey Biography." Inspirational Christians. November 29, 2014. https://www. inspirationalchristians.org/biography/thomas-dorsey.

Moore, Richard. "The History of Transportation on the Mississippi River: Part Two." Center for Global Environmental Education. Hamline University. 2001. https://cgee.hamline.edu/rivers/Resources/Voices/transportation2.htm.

Open Vault. "March on Washington for Jobs and Freedom; Part 7 of 17." March on Washington. Special Collections. WGBH Media Library and Archives. August 28, 1963. http://openvault.wgbh.org/catalog/A_FDC80454052747988DEA7F89F4D23B9F.

Pacyga, Dominic A. "South Side." Encyclopedia of Chicago. 2005. http://www.encyclopedia.chicagohistory.org/pages/1177.html.

Scott, Mike. "1963: Mahalia Jackson lifts her voice, inspires MLK's 'I Have a Dream' speech." NOLA.com. August 27, 2017. https://www.nola.com/300/2017/08/mahalia_jackson_i_have_a_dream.html.

Rock & Roll Hall of Fame. "Sister Rosetta Tharpe." Last accessed July 11, 2019. https://www.rockhall.com/inductees/sister-rosetta-tharpe.

Smithsonian National Museum of American History. "River Towns, River Networks." Inland Waterways. On the Water. Last accessed July 11, 2019. http://americanhistory.si.edu/onthewater/exhibition/4_4.html.

Stroud, Hubert B. "Mississippi River." Encyclopedia of Arkansas. Last updated April 17, 2017. http://www.encyclopediaofarkansas.net/encyclopedia/entry-detail.aspx?entryID=2648.

Terkel, Studs. "Studs and Mahalia Jackson." May 15, 2012. In *The Story*, podcast. MP3 audio.

Whitman, Alden. "Mahalia Jackson, Gospel Singer, and a Civil Rights Symbol, Dies." *New York Times*, January 28, 1972. https://archive.nytimes.com/www.nytimes.com/learning/general/onthisday/bday/1026.html.

Wolfe, Charles K. *Mahalia Jackson, Gospel Singer.* New York: Chelsea House Publishers, 1990.

Further Reading

Jackson, Mahalia, with Evan McLeod Wylie. *Movin' On Up.* New York: Hawthorn Books, 1966.

Kramer, Barbara. *Mahalia Jackson: The Voice of Gospel and Civil Rights.* Berkeley Heights, NJ: Enslow Publishers, 2003.

Wolfe, Charles K. *Mahalia Jackson, Gospel Singer.* New York: Chelsea House Publishers, 1990.

About the Author

Denise Lewis Patrick is a native of Natchitoches, Louisiana. She graduated with a BA in journalism from Northwestern State University of Louisiana and holds an MFA from the University of New Orleans.

She's written fiction and nonfiction for every age group, including board books, picture books, biographies, middle grade historical fiction, and young adult fiction. Her poetry has been published in several online literary magazines. She's volunteered as a mentor to young writers in a local after-school program and is currently an adjunct professor in the First-Year Writing Program at Montclair State University.

Her most recent works include the biography *A Girl Named Rosa*, the historical fiction novels *No Ordinary Sound* and *Never Stop Singing*, and the middle grade novel *Finding Someplace*.

In her spare time, she writes poetry and makes cloth dolls. She is also the married mother of adult sons.